bearing

DEVOTIONS FOR LENT 2016

 AUGSBURG FORTRESS

Minneapolis

BEARING FRUIT
Devotions for Lent 2016

ISBN 978-1-5064-0061-7

Writers: David L. Miller (February 10–17; March 19–26), Anne Edison-Albright (February 18–March 3), Harvard Stephens Jr. (March 4–18)
Editors: Suzanne Burke, Laurie J. Hanson
Cover design: Laurie Ingram
Interior design: Eileen Engebretson

The paper used in this publication meets the minimum requirements of American National Standard for Information Sciences—Permanence of Paper for Printed Library Materials, ANSI Z329.48-1984.

Manufactured in the U.S.A.

16 15   1 2 3 4 5 6 7 8 9 10

Welcome

"Bear fruit," says the letter to the Colossians, not as a burden but as our great joy. As our roots go deeper into the word and we soak up God's saving grace, we grow and bear the fruit of living new lives in Christ—faith, forgiveness, healing, hope, joy, and love. This fruit invites others to experience God's love and sends the peace of Christ into the world.

For each day in Lent 2016, *Bearing Fruit* offers an evocative image, a reading from Colossians, a quotation to ponder, a reflection, and a prayer. Colossians is one of the New Testament letters read in worship during this liturgical year (year C of the Revised Common Lectionary). The writers bring their unique voices and pastoral wisdom to these texts, and also offer the voices of other witnesses in the quotations they have chosen for the "To ponder" section for each day.

Images provide another way into these texts. Take time to wonder about the images. What do they say that words cannot?

May the rich, new life given to you through Christ bear fruit as you journey through the days of Lent toward the Easter feast.

—The editors

Colossians 1:1-2

Paul, an apostle of Christ Jesus by the will of God, and Timothy our brother,

To the saints and faithful brothers and sisters in Christ in Colossae:

Grace to you and peace from God our Father.

To ponder

Lord, send me a surprise. One that catches me off guard and makes me wonder. . . . Send me a resurrection when everything looks dead and buried. Send me light when the night seems too long. Send me spring when the cold and frozen season seems endless. Send me a new idea when my mind is empty. Send me a thing to do when I am just waiting around. Send me a new friend when I am alone. Send me peace when I'm afraid. Send me a future when it looks hopeless. Send me your resurrection when I die, Jesus. —Herbert Brokering, *Surprise Me, Jesus*

Ready to go

Every day is a journey, Holy One, a journey of hope.

I remember all those reporting trips, dragging my bags through airports to cities and peoples unknown to me, knowing only that it was you, through your church, who sent me. I went, always knowing you would find me in places I had never known or imagined. You taught me to live in expectation. I never knew where, how, or when you would open my eyes to see and my ears to hear you. I just knew it would happen, and it always did.

That's the way you are. You hunger to be known. You communicate not this or that idea about you, but the grace and peace, the fullness of Love you are.

No longer must I hustle through airports. Those days are done. But each day is its own journey, and I still don't know where or how or when you will surprise me.

I know only that you are the Mystery of this Love who seeks me in every face I see and every place I go. So let the journey begin. I carry no bag, only a heart filled with hope.

Prayer

Thanks for the journey of my life, Holy One. You have surprised me many times. Surprise me again today. Amen.

February 11

Colossians 1:3-5a

In our prayers for you we always thank God, the Father of our Lord Jesus Christ, for we have heard of your faith in Christ Jesus and of the love that you have for all the saints, because of the hope laid up for you in heaven.

To ponder

But the ultimate reason for our hope is not to be found at all in what we want, wish for, and wait for; the ultimate reason for our hope is that we are wanted and wished for and waited for. . . . We are accepted and received, as a mother takes her children into her arms and comforts them. God is our last hope because we are God's first love. . . . God is waiting for the homecoming of those he has created. —Jürgen Moltmann, *The Source of Life*

The colors of Love

Two words fill the heart. They are absolutely necessary and totally inadequate: *Thank you*.

Thank you, Holy One, for the exquisite hope that fills my life with light and color, beauty and joy. My hope is to know union, total and complete, with you who are Love Incomprehensible.

Nothing else will do. Nothing else quite satisfies the soul. You made us for this. Our hearts long to see and know you beyond the gray shadows of our earthly vision.

We have seen your face in the grace of our Lord Jesus Christ. And we know the Love in him is you, Holy One, a Love with neither beginning nor end, a Love drawing us home to you that our lives, too, may shine with the colors of you who are Love.

This hope, laid up for us in heaven, fills us with love for you and all you have made, for sun and moon, for the souls we meet and the distant stars, knowing all that is comes from the Love you are, and knowing you will not rest until all that is shines with the colors of your life.

Prayer

God, fulfill the hope of our hearts to know you and be filled with the love that shines in the face of our brother, Jesus. Amen.

February 12

Colossians 1:5b-6
You have heard of this hope before in the word of the truth, the gospel that has come to you. Just as it is bearing fruit and growing in the whole world, so it has been bearing fruit among yourselves from the day you heard it and truly comprehended the grace of God.

To ponder
Our DNA is divine. The divine indwelling is never earned by any behavior whatsoever or any ritual, but only *recognized* and *realized* . . . and fallen in love with. . . . In prayer, we merely keep returning the divine gaze, and we become its reflection, almost in spite of ourselves. —Richard Rohr, *The Naked Now*

The fruit of life

They are only figs on a branch, but I see ecstasy, an explosion of life and beauty. They sit in the sun, soak up the rain, and the power of being within them bursts the bondage of branch and stem to bear fruit that delights the eye and feeds body and soul.

We are like the figs, Holy One. Your life flows through our souls and bursts into being as we bask in the warmth of the Incomprehensible Love you are.

Your grace embraces all we are, even the most broken and shameful places, enveloping us like the air, warming the heart and awakening your life and love within. To know such grace is to know you, Loving Mystery, the one whom no mind or heart can encompass.

But there is a knowing for us, a heart-to-heart awareness that you want us. You hunger for us. The Love you are fills our brother, Jesus, seeking to warm our hearts until they explode with life and love, beauty and joy, bearing the fruit of your life through the work of our hands.

We don't make it happen. We just sit in the sun and soak up the rain.

Prayer

God, teach us to sit in the warmth of your presence that our lives may bear the fruit of justice and joy. Amen.

Colossians 1:7-8

This you learned from Epaphras, our beloved fellow servant. He is a faithful minister of Christ on your behalf, and he has made known to us your love in the Spirit.

To ponder

Christian life is a commitment to love, to give birth to God in one's own life and to become midwives of divinity in this evolving cosmos. . . . We are born out of love, we exist in love and we are destined for eternal love. Instead of developing faster computers, smaller chips or artificial means of new life, it is time to reinvent ourselves in love. —Ilia Delio, "Love at the Heart of the Universe," *Oneing*

Madison's ministry

Madison is my teacher. She is six, and she has a new lesson for me every Sunday. She hunts me down whether I am in the sanctuary, the sacristy, or my office, often with several other children in tow.

Brown eyes flashing, she turns her face up to me and wants to be hugged or picked up. She is getting a bit big for scooping up. But she wants the touch of the love that binds us, the joy we find in knowing that we love each other—and we love each other a lot.

Once in a while, she brings me a gift, but the real gift is the connection we share that teaches me week by week what life is about.

Madison is a good teacher, a faithful minister of Christ. After six decades of living, I am beginning to understand. The life to which you call us, Holy One, is about being connected with each other in common hope, love, and struggle to live the Love you are, ministering to each other amid the stuff of daily life.

It is not about me but about *us*, joined in the love your Spirit awakens in our souls.

Prayer

Stir us to live for others, God, sharing the love your Spirit stirs in our hearts. Amen.

February 14 / Lent 1

Colossians 1:9-10

For this reason, since the day we heard it, we have not ceased praying for you and asking that you may be filled with the knowledge of God's will in all spiritual wisdom and understanding, so that you may lead lives worthy of the Lord, fully pleasing to him, as you bear fruit in every good work and as you grow in the knowledge of God.

To ponder

Love is not a duty we grimly perform. It has to do with delight in God and other people even at its hardest. . . . Delight in love is the gift of God, God loving in us. It is not something we can grit our teeth and do. . . . Our growing in love is a continuous movement into God's [limitless] love. —Roberta Bondi, *To Love as God Loves*

Lost in love

Sunlight awakens my soul as I drive down the street. The world is alive, but more wondrously, so am I. Love surges and fills every pore of my being. I am in love with everything and everyone I see. I am one with you, engulfed and soaked to the bone in the Love flowing from your unfathomable heart.

This joy wasn't there a moment ago, but now I know you beyond any idea I ever learned about you. And I know what you are doing under the sun, a knowing that warms me on this winter morning.

All that is, all I see, every soul I meet is to be brought into union with the Love you are, joined with you and all else, one great sharing in Love.

Your will is that we be as Christ, a blessed union of Spirit and created matter, your love filling and infusing all so that everything everywhere shimmers with light and color, shining like the sun on this crystal day.

This is the deep desire of your heart, your holy dream, and today my great joy, the fruit of knowing you.

Prayer

Fill our lives, God, that we may bear rich fruit, coloring this world with the splendor of your presence. Amen.

February 15

Colossians 1:11-12

May you be made strong with all the strength that comes from his glorious power, and may you be prepared to endure everything with patience, while joyfully giving thanks to the Father, who has enabled you to share in the inheritance of the saints in the light.

To ponder

Life tears us apart, but through those wounds, if we have tended them, love may enter us. It may be the love of someone you have lost. It may be the love of your own spirit for the self that at times you think you hate. However it comes though, in all these—of all these and yet more than they, so much more—there burns the abiding love of God. . . . No one can say what names or forms God might take. —Christian Wiman, *My Bright Abyss*

The face of power

The boy was only nine but so powerful. He was going to Rome to visit the pope. It was his dying wish, but his cancer was too aggressive and he couldn't make the trip. The medical staff at Lurie Children's Hospital in Chicago suggested another idea. Maybe Cardinal Francis George could visit him.

The cardinal could only call because he, too, was dying. But it was enough. The two were connected heart to heart in common hope, love, and shared suffering.

Weeks later the boy asked how the cardinal was. "He is about to go on the same journey as you," the chaplain answered. "Please tell him I will be waiting for him in heaven," the boy said.

He was only nine, just a boy, but so full of your power, Holy One, the power to bless and make whole, the power that fills us with beauty and strength.

The strength you give is not armor plating against the wounds of life. It has nothing to do with militaristic might or force. You give strength to endure, to hold fast to who we are and what you call us to do—blessing and forgiving, helping and healing—like nine-year-olds.

Prayer

Strengthen our souls, God, to do the good that reveals your compassion for all creation. Amen.

Colossians 1:13-14

He has rescued us from the power of darkness and transferred us into the kingdom of his beloved Son, in whom we have redemption, the forgiveness of sins.

To ponder

We have been seen by God from all eternity and seen as unique, special, precious beings. . . . From all eternity, long before you were born and became part of history, you existed in God's heart. Long before your parents admired you or your friends acknowledged your gifts or your teachers, colleagues, and employers encouraged you, you were already "chosen." The eyes of love had seen you as precious, as of infinite beauty, and as of eternal value. —Henri J. M. Nouwen, *Life of the Beloved*

The time of day

Morning comes, but too few know what time it is. Everywhere I go I see faces stressed and anxious, afraid of tomorrow while needlessly bearing the weight of yesterday's wounds and guilt. Each struggling to find their way, little knowing they are loved beyond their wildest imagination.

Difficulties at home, work, or school, failures to be what they want to be—these and more steal truth and joy from them, leaving them lifeless.

They do not know that each day is new, not just a repetition of what came before. Light pours over the weary world with each sunrise. Joy lies waiting to surprise in faces and places, laughter and learning.

All that you are, O Christ, is present with each new dawn. You share the belovedness that fills you as you live in communion with the Loving Mystery you call *Father*.

When this truth washes over us, our hearts grow light, colors are brighter, and new faces hold promise not threat. Dry, lifeless places in our souls come alive. Laughter bubbles from our lips, and our minds reflexively find gratitude, no longer dwelling among dark thoughts that sour our souls.

It's a new day; the beloved Son's kingdom comes every day.

Prayer

God, open our ears to hear the truth that we are your beloved. Amen.

February 17

Colossians 1:15-16

He is the image of the invisible God, the firstborn of all creation; for in him all things in heaven and on earth were created, things visible and invisible, whether thrones or dominions or rulers or powers—all things have been created through him and for him.

To ponder

For the world and time are the dance of the Lord in emptiness. The silence of the spheres is the music of a wedding feast. . . . No despair of ours can alter the reality of things, or stain the joy of the cosmic dance which is always there. Indeed, we are in the midst of it, and it is in the midst of us, for it beats in our very blood, whether we know it or not. . . . We are invited to forget ourselves on purpose, cast our awful solemnity to the winds and join in the general dance. —Thomas Merton, *New Seeds of Contemplation*

The cosmic dance

Our telescopic eyes penetrate distant space, and we stagger at the beauty and immensity of a universe we can barely imagine. We see nearly to the dawn of time—13.7 billion years, I am told.

That is when the cosmos exploded into existence from an infinitesimal point so dense no light could escape. From this come 200 billion galaxies each with 100 billion stars, most of which make our sun look puny.

There are more stars in the sky than there are grains of sand on all the beaches and deserts on earth. And every second the universe grows and new stars are born.

All of it, every atom and galaxy, is made in and for Christ. Each springs to life from the joy of your divine heart, Loving Mystery. Each is created in love and destined to be united in a great, cosmic dance of peace and beauty where all is one.

The universe is one great story, your story, Holy One. It begins in the desire of your heart and ends in a dance of light and love where each thing takes its place in the Love you are— glistening with the glory of your life.

Prayer

God, may the wonder of the night sky humble our hearts and move us to joy and praise. Amen.

February 18

Colossians 1:17
He himself is before all things, and in him all things hold
together.

To ponder
There were tens of thousands of pilgrims, from all over the
world. They were of all colors, from blue-eyed blonds to black-
skinned Africans. But we were all participating in the same
ritual, displaying a spirit of unity and brotherhood that my
experiences in America had led me to believe never could exist
between the white and the non-white. . . . I could see from this,
that perhaps if white Americans could accept the Oneness
of God, then perhaps, too, they could accept in reality the
Oneness of Man—and cease to measure, and hinder, and harm

others in terms of their "differences" in color. —Alex Haley, *The Autobiography of Malcolm X*

Unity in diversity

Malcolm X's experience of the *hajj*, Islam's holy pilgrimage to Mecca, was transformative. Before then, he'd found it difficult to imagine any true unity or cooperation between white and black people was possible. In Islam, there is the idea of the *ummah*, a community of faith that transcends race, class, language, and all other barriers. When you stand shoulder-to-shoulder with people in prayer, you have a sense of connection that is deeper than human similarities or differences.

In Christianity, our image of unity in diversity is the body of Christ. Every part of the body is different, important, and beloved, and every part belongs to the body just as much as every other part. A body that diverse, that vast, and that inclusive is bound to be a little unruly. There is deep connectedness, yes, but also conflict. And yet we are one. Jesus holds all things together.

Prayer

God of all, we give thanks for our diversity and pray for love that unites us with other Christians, with other people of faith, and with all creation. Amen.

Colossians 1:18

He is the head of the body, the church; he is the beginning, the firstborn from the dead, so that he might come to have first place in everything.

To ponder

I truly believed that my time was finished. . . . I planned my funeral. . . . I was convinced this would be my last Christmas, my last anniversary, the winding down with the family and friends that I love. . . . Suddenly I realized that the love notes that before had to disrupt my awareness in order for me to perceive them, required no such violence. In the quiet solitude of winding down is the ocean roar of love. —Bruce H. Kramer, *We Know How This Ends: Living While Dying*

First things, last things

"I really feel," the older man said, "like I'm starting to live parts of my life a second time. Like as I get older, events from my youth and childhood are happening again. It's as though my life is a novel, and as it is coming to an end, the Author is drawing parallels, revealing foreshadowing, and repeating key themes."

"What's that like for you?"

"Familiar! And I've always appreciated good writing. I'm looking forward to my birth."

Prayer

God, when we encounter the new birth that is death, sometimes we are at peace, but sometimes we are angry, and sometimes we are sad or afraid. Let us hear the ocean roar of your love, Lord. We give thanks for your Son, Jesus Christ, and his birth from death into resurrection. In times of first things and last things, God, you have been, are, and always will be. Amen.

February 20

Colossians 1:19-20

For in him all the fullness of God was pleased to dwell, and
through him God was pleased to reconcile to himself all things,
whether on earth or in heaven, by making peace through the
blood of his cross.

To ponder

The prim, apocalyptic Christian man smiled. Then he laughed
out loud. The Latvian woman started laughing then.... I started
laughing too. The three of us sat there in hysterics. And when
we were done, the man reached over and patted the back of my
hand, smiling gently. The Latvian woman leaned in close to me,
into my Soviet air space, and she beamed. I leaned forward so
that our foreheads touched for just a second.... Now I felt like

I was sitting with my cousins on a plane eight miles up, a plane that was going to make it home. And it made me so happy that I suddenly thought, this is plenty of miracle for me to rest in now.
—Anne Lamott, *Traveling Mercies*

Making peace

"World peace" is kind of a punch line, right? If someone is granted three wishes, and one of them is world peace, you know there's some kind of joke or terrible plot twist coming.

And yet the full reconciliation of all things, on earth and in heaven, is what God does through Jesus. God is pleased to do it! It is a joy to bring peace to all the world.

The big miracle of peacemaking happened, paradoxically, through the violent act of Jesus' crucifixion and death. Only God could overturn something violent and use it to bring reconciling grace, love, and forgiveness to all people.

The daily miracle of peacemaking is happening all around us—world peace, happening everywhere, right now. Even in airplanes eight miles up, where unlikely friendships can form.

Prayer

God, we pray for peace in our hearts, peace in our homes, peace with friends and strangers, peace on earth and in heaven. Thank you for daily miracles of peace, big and small, and for the greatest peacemaking miracle, Jesus. Amen.

February 21 / Lent 2

Colossians 1:21-23a

And you who were once estranged and hostile in mind, doing evil deeds, he has now reconciled in his fleshly body through death, so as to present you holy and blameless and irreproachable before him—provided that you continue securely established and steadfast in the faith, without shifting from the hope promised by the gospel that you heard, which has been proclaimed to every creature under heaven.

To ponder

This inability to reconcile myself to death has not been good for me. I visit Saint James like an addict drops by a crack house. For a fix. To deaden the pain, by losing myself momentarily in the fantasy that she lives, and that we will be together again. . . . If I were the kind of person who could believe, I would believe. But I'm not that kind of person. —Dan Savage, *This American Life*

God does the work

The truth is that none of us can reconcile ourselves to death, and none of us is the kind of person who can believe on our own. That's what makes Dan Savage's story about his mother's death so heartbreaking and why it rings so true. Death *is* real, and it changes things in real ways. We are, and should be, hostile to death and estranged from it.

The good news is that we don't have to reconcile ourselves to death; Christ has reconciled us to God through death. God does the work, even the work of giving us faith when faith seems impossible. The heartbreak is still real, but the hope is real too.

Even if you shift a bit (or a lot) from hope to hopelessness and back again, the gospel is proclaimed for you (and every other creature under heaven too).

Prayer

God, give us hope when we feel hopeless. Give us faith when we can't believe in you. Reconcile us to you and to the world and to each other. Amen.

February 22

Colossians 1:23b-24

I, Paul, became a servant of this gospel.

I am now rejoicing in my sufferings for your sake, and in my flesh I am completing what is lacking in Christ's afflictions for the sake of his body, that is, the church.

To ponder

I refuse to have my scars hidden or trivialized behind lambswool or silicone gel. I refuse to be reduced in my own eyes or in the eyes of others from warrior to mere victim, simply because it might render me a fraction more acceptable or less dangerous to the still complacent, those who believe that if you cover up a problem it ceases to exist. —Audre Lorde, *The Cancer Journals*

Warrior victim, rejoicing sufferer

Most people who live long enough to enjoy life also pick up some scars along the way. I got my first when I was four and a half years old: a long white line across my belly where a tumor was removed. I showed that scar to everyone I met. "This," I announced proudly, "is my scar. It means I am very brave."

Faced with the wounded, scarred body of Jesus Christ, early Christians had a choice. They could try to cover it up and pretend there was no death and no suffering, only glorious resurrection. Or they could embrace the whole truth of Jesus: his death *and* his resurrection, his human suffering *and* his divine triumph.

It would be more comfortable to hide those scars. It would be easier if there wasn't so much paradox at the heart of our faith! But in that easy comfort, we would lose the essential message of the cross: God is always where you'd least expect an all-powerful being to be. God is with you in your suffering.

Prayer

God, heal us, be with us, give us courage. Help us find you in unlikely places and difficult times. Amen.

Colossians 1:25-26

I became [the church's] servant according to God's commission that was given to me for you, to make the word of God fully known, the mystery that has been hidden throughout the ages and generations but has now been revealed to his saints.

To ponder

I can see clearly now
The rain is gone.
—Johnny Nash, "I Can See Clearly Now"

Hidden and revealed

Are we being promised too much here? What about "for now we see in a mirror, dimly" and "now I know only in part" (1 Corinthians 13:12)? Can the mystery of God really be fully known, fully revealed?

If you wear glasses, you may remember what it was like to put them on for the first time, look at a tree, and suddenly be able to discern individual, distinct leaves. You may still get that feeling sometimes when you clean your glasses and realize the world is bright and crisp again. If you've experienced depression, you may have had the experience of the world noticeably, visibly lightening and sharpening when the depression lifts. When things that were hidden are revealed, we notice. We see a difference.

Human moments of clarity can be fleeting. God's full revelation in Jesus is eternal, which means it's always there, even when our vision is obscured. The Son is always shining.

Prayer

God, thank you for fully revealing your love and grace in Jesus. Help us see your Son! Amen.

February 24

Colossians 1:27
To them God chose to make known how great among the Gentiles are the riches of the glory of this mystery, which is Christ in you, the hope of glory.

To ponder
Christ be with me, Christ within me, Christ behind me, Christ before me, Christ beside me, Christ to win me, Christ to comfort and restore me, Christ beneath me, Christ above me, Christ in quiet, Christ in danger, Christ in hearts of all that love me, Christ in mouth of friend and stranger. —"I Bind unto Myself Today" (St. Patrick's Breastplate)

The mystery of Christ in you

The kids at church are pretty well trained, now, to answer the question "Where is Jesus?" They just start pointing in all directions. They point up to heaven. They point to themselves, to their own hearts. They point to the pastor and the people and the musicians in the band. They point out, way out, out the doors of the church and into the world. Some of the really advanced ones even remember to point to the communion bread and wine, and to the baptismal font. They know "Jesus is everywhere!"

There is something about singing "Christ be with me, Christ within me, Christ behind me . . . ," though, that moves that truth from the realm of "children's message obviousness" right back into "mystery," in the form of a lump in my throat and tears running down my face.

How can this be? How can God possibly love us this much?

Prayer

God, it is hard sometimes to imagine the depth of your love, the constancy of your presence, the abundance of your grace. Thank you. Amen.

February 25

Colossians 1:28-29

It is he whom we proclaim, warning everyone and teaching everyone in all wisdom, so that we may present everyone mature in Christ. For this I toil and struggle with all the energy that he powerfully inspires within me.

To ponder

I think the real clue to the tameness of a preacher is the difficulty one finds in telling unpleasant truths to people whom one has learned to love. To speak the truth in love is a difficult, and sometimes an almost impossible, achievement. —Reinhold Niebuhr, *Leaves from the Notebook of a Tamed Cynic*

Tameness and toil

Proclaiming Christ is a dangerous thing in many parts of the world today. In some places, the danger is a matter of life and death.

For Christians who live in North America and other parts of the world where there is not violent religious conflict, the danger is in complacency. Some of it could be the tameness that Niebuhr describes: it's hard to tell difficult truths to people you love. Some of it could be the apathy that comes from comfort, or from grieving for a previous era when congregations were larger.

If there is a need for toil, for work to be done (and there is), then God will powerfully inspire the energy needed to do it. That's what the Holy Spirit does. The Spirit comes into our tame, complacent, apathetic, and grieving hearts and gives us the joy we need to move forward. The Spirit can even give us the rare, but crucial, gift of courage to speak the truth in love. The people we love need to hear the truth of the gospel, even if it is difficult, even if it makes them uncomfortable.

Prayer

God, we pray for Christians around the world facing real and terrible danger every day. Protect their lives and give them hope. Give hope and energy to all congregations. Send your Spirit to comfort the afflicted and afflict the comfortable. Amen.

Colossians 2:1

For I want you to know how much I am struggling for you, and for those in Laodicea, and for all who have not seen me face to face.

To ponder

If life cannot be destroyed for good, then neither can history be brought entirely to a halt. A secret streamlet trickles on beneath the heavy cover of inertia and pseudo-events, slowly and inconspicuously undercutting it. It may be a long process, but one day it must happen: the cover will no longer hold and will start to crack. —Václav Havel, "Dear Dr. Husák"

Hidden struggle

When you tour the sites where walls fell, where people brought down Communism with candles and songs and linked arms across old churchyards, you get the feeling that it could not have possibly happened the way it did. "Is not possible," our Slovak friends would say.

The daughter of a Slovak pastor knew she could never grow up to be a teacher, because people associated with religion were banned from having any influence on children or public life. This is just how it was; this was reality. And then reality changed. Lutheran schools reopened, and she became a teacher.

In between those two realities, there was struggle. Most of it was hidden from view, underground and secret. When the cover started to crack and people took to the streets with candles, it looked like a spring had welled up out of nowhere. But the struggle had been there, beneath the surface, long before.

When you tour those sites where walls fell, where people marched and sang with candles, where they filled churches in defiant hope, you may get to meet someone face-to-face who was part of that struggle. With God's help they did something impossible.

Prayer

God, with you all things are possible. Bless all who struggle for freedom. Amen.

February 27

Colossians 2:2-3

I want their hearts to be encouraged and united in love, so that they may have all the riches of assured understanding and have the knowledge of God's mystery, that is, Christ himself, in whom are hidden all the treasures of wisdom and knowledge.

To ponder

So I believe that one day
    the sun will shine again, calm on the Indian Ocean . . .
And this poison of the moon that suffering has infused in my
    veins will cease disturbing me forever.

One day,
    life will be flooded with sun.
And it will be like a new childhood shining for everyone.
—Noémia da Sousa, "Poem of Distant Childhood"

Encouraged

When people are encouraged and united in love, they can get through just about any difficult time together. The "together" part is important. Much of our suffering and pain we experience alone. Even when we reach out for help, as we should, there are some experiences that can't be shared. But encouragement is most powerful when it is shared. The more it is shared, the more power it gains.

Make it a point today to offer encouragement to others, and see what happens.

Prayer

Gracious God, unite our congregations in love, and encourage them to serve you and others in wonderful ways. Unite our communities in love, and encourage all community organizations to serve you and others in wonderful ways. Unite our nation in love; encourage all elected leaders to serve you and others in wonderful ways. Unite our world in love; encourage every one of us to serve you and others in wonderful ways. Amen.

February 28 / Lent 3

Colossians 2:4-5

I am saying this so that no one may deceive you with plausible arguments. For though I am absent in body, yet I am with you in spirit, and I rejoice to see your morale and the firmness of your faith in Christ.

To ponder

Failing to fetch me at first keep encouraged,
Missing me one place search another,
I stop somewhere waiting for you.
—Walt Whitman, "Song of Myself"

Keep encouraged

Something was missing. All the desks were cleaned and in place. There were inspirational posters on the wall—quotes from Eleanor Roosevelt, Gandhi, Cesar Chavez, Martin Luther King Jr., Albert Einstein. Also Bob Dylan. The classroom library was well stocked and organized. But something was missing.

How would her students know, really know, how much she cared about them? That she cared about them right now, before even meeting them, and that she'd continue to care about them long after they left her classroom? It's one thing to know that someone cares when you are standing there looking at them. It's another thing for that feeling of love and well-being to stay with you when that person is out of sight.

She thought about her favorite Walt Whitman quote and how it made her feel like all the people she loved, even people who had died, were somewhere, just around the next corner, just out of sight, cheering for her, urging her on.

She made another poster.

Prayer

God, thank you for teachers and the encouragement they give. Most of all, thank you for our greatest teacher, Jesus Christ, in whose name we pray. Amen.

Colossians 2:6-7

As you therefore have received Christ Jesus the Lord, continue to live your lives in him, rooted and built up in him and established in the faith, just as you were taught, abounding in thanksgiving.

To ponder

I learned from my mother how to love
the living . . . I learned to save jars
large enough to hold fruit salad for a whole grieving household . . .
I learned to attend viewings even if I didn't know the deceased . . .
I learned that whatever we say means nothing,
what anyone will remember is that we came.
—Julia Kasdorf, "What I Learned from My Mother"

Rooted and taught

As children our roots are extra thirsty. You can almost see the little white feelers of new growth coming off of a child's fingertips as she reaches out to touch, taste, or experience something new. She's a little hesitant at first, maybe, but with encouragement from a trusted adult, she dives into that warm earth, soaking up as much as she can, learning, learning, learning with great joy and delight.

As adults, sometimes we are a little root-bound. Our growth is curbed, choked off by the limits of our containers. Transplants and other changes are good for us, but also scary and vulnerable times.

There's no going back to the days when our roots were first forming, but there's also nothing quite like being that trusted adult, the one who is there helping someone else's first roots form. We are the teachers now, the ones who point to the bright sun, to the warm earth, to the cool water and say, "It's safe, it's good. You can grow here!"

Thanks be to God!

Prayer

Gracious God, thank you for the life-giving lessons we learned from our mothers, our fathers, and all those who were and are like parents to us. Guide us in teaching and encouraging the children in our lives about your love. Amen.

March 1

Colossians 2:8

See to it that no one takes you captive through philosophy and empty deceit, according to human tradition, according to the elemental spirits of the universe, and not according to Christ.

To ponder

You are so young, so before all beginning, and I want to beg you . . . to be patient toward all that is unsolved in your heart and to try to love the *questions themselves* like locked rooms and like books that are written in a very foreign tongue. Do not now seek answers, which cannot be given you because you would not be able to live them. . . . *Live* the questions now. Perhaps you will then gradually, without noticing it, live along some distant day into the answer. —Rainer Maria Rilke, *Letters to a Young Poet*

Living Christ, living questions

"See to it that no one takes you captive." But how can we tell when we're being deceived? How are we supposed to know what is human tradition and what is Christ?

The teachings of Jesus are actually quite different from the teachings of the world. Jesus regularly turns our expectations upside down, especially when it comes to power dynamics. He preferred to associate himself with the outcasts of society: criminals, women, collaborators, foreigners, children, and people who were hungry, sick, and homeless. Teachings that dehumanize or oppress people who have been disempowered are teachings of the world, not Jesus.

Another way to differentiate between worldly teaching and Jesus' teaching is how well the teaching tolerates ambiguity. Jesus taught in parables; sometimes they help to clarify his points, and usually they raise even more questions. As disciples, we need to get comfortable with a certain amount of uncertainty. Human tradition wants to answer it all, easily, right now. Living with Christ means living the questions and not settling for easy answers.

Prayer

God, help us discern your teaching. When we are frustrated with our questions, give us patience to wrestle with them, pray about them, and live with them. Amen.

March 2

Colossians 2:9-10

For in him the whole fullness of deity dwells bodily, and you have come to fullness in him, who is the head of every ruler and authority.

To ponder

It was only a smile, nothing more. It didn't make everything all right. It didn't make *anything* all right. Only a smile. A tiny thing. A leaf in the woods, shaking in the wake of a startled bird's flight.

But I'll take it. With open arms. Because when spring comes, it melts the snow one flake at a time, and maybe I just witnessed the first flake melting. —Khaled Hosseini, *The Kite Runner*

Embodied

Can you imagine Jesus' smile?

The idea that God would choose to be human, that God would lower God's self to put on flesh and deal with all the indignity that comes with having a body—including the violence of birth and death—that idea was a scandal, a stumbling block to the ancient world. The body was just a container, and a leaky, unreliable one at that. What would God want with a body?

Can you imagine Jesus' smile?

Prayer

Thank you for our bodies, God. Thank you for smiles, for open arms, for the indescribable joy of being embodied beings. Thank you for choosing to become fully embodied with us. It's wonderful, isn't it? Amen.

March 3

Colossians 2:11-12

In him also you were circumcised with a spiritual circumcision, by putting off the body of the flesh in the circumcision of Christ; when you were buried with him in baptism, you were also raised with him through faith in the power of God, who raised him from the dead.

To ponder

I am the seed that grows the wheat . . .
Before I grow, I go deep down:
I die, the dark earth underground.
Water gives me life again,
      And I become the golden grain . . .
And I am the water went under the ground

To turn the whole world upside down,
  To bring the dead to life.
—Walter Wangerin Jr., *Water, Come Down!*

The world turned upside down

I feel a little strange telling parents I'm burying their children when I baptize them. I am especially careful about using that language with parents who have had previous experience of burying children who have died.

Hannah, even though she died before she was born, was baptized by our tears and received immediately into the grace and love of God. She was buried, and she will rise again with Christ.

Avery, up front at the font in the congregation with her parents and sponsors and grandparents and everyone saying, "We will! We will!" was baptized by water and the Word and the Holy Spirit. She was buried, too, in that moment—her sins died and were washed away. Every day of her life, her sins will be buried by her baptism, and she will live forgiven and free.

Someday, like all of us, Avery will die. She will rise again, with Christ and her sister Hannah, on the last day.

It feels a little strange to say it, a little upside down. But we bury when we baptize. And it is a good thing. Amen.

Prayer

God, bless us when we mourn and when we rejoice. Bury our sin and raise us to new life with you. Amen.

March 4

Colossians 2:13-15

And when you were dead in trespasses and the uncircumcision of your flesh, God made you alive together with him, when he forgave us all our trespasses, erasing the record that stood against us with its legal demands. He set this aside, nailing it to the cross. He disarmed the rulers and authorities and made a public example of them, triumphing over them in it.

To ponder

Having a public life is as fundamental to our humanness, to our well-being, as having a private life; without the two halves, life cannot be whole. The God who cares about our private lives is concerned with our public lives as well. This is a God who calls us into relationship not only with family and friends, but with strangers scattered across the face of the earth, a God who says again and again, "We are all in this together." —Parker J. Palmer, *The Company of Strangers*

Living together in grace

The rulers and authorities who tried to suppress Jesus' message had no idea that God's grace could be so powerful, able to overcome the divisions among Jews and Gentiles. The forgiveness we receive today through the love of Christ continues to set us free to reach beyond the social, cultural, and political divisions that separate us from one another.

Celebrate what this amazing grace makes possible in our world today. Learn more about those all around us who show how friendship and dialogue work together to dismantle the persistent power of hatred and mistrust. Imagine how you can work with others to create safe places for celebrating visions of justice and reconciliation that offer alternatives to violence in our homes, neighborhoods, and within the global community.

Prayer

The power of your love renews our bodies and souls, refreshes our spirits, and restores our hope in your gifts of grace. Be with us, wondrous God, in every good endeavor, so that we will find joy and peace in this world and in the world to come. Amen.

March 5

Colossians 2:16-17

Therefore do not let anyone condemn you in matters of food and drink or of observing festivals, new moons, or sabbaths. These are only a shadow of what is to come, but the substance belongs to Christ.

To ponder

"A couple of years ago . . . I almost lost my family because of my drinking. I mistreated my wife and my children, especially my oldest son. But you and your wife spent a lot of time with him at a critical moment in his life. . . . Shortly after that time I went to AA, and I've been sober ever since. Because of you and your wife, I still have a relationship with my son. I've never been able to thank you, but I'm thanking you now." . . .

This alcoholic, abusing, untrustworthy man had just shown this arrogant, self-righteous snob the meaning of grace.
—Michael Yaconelli, *Dangerous Wonder*

A new kind of freedom

An empty plate. An empty cup. An empty heart. There are many signs of hunger and human need. Our efforts to satisfy our deepest longings can expose our greatest fears. In our weaknesses we can make foolish choices and develop habits and addictions that diminish our dignity and weaken our faith.

God gives us the gift of compassion so we can care for each other in the manner of our Lord Jesus Christ. His love grounds us in a reality overflowing with a new kind of freedom. We are free to embrace each other and admit our own faults and failures as we care for our mutual wounds of body, mind, and spirit.

Our human frailties no longer have to drive us apart. There is room at the table for all who hunger, all who hurt, and all who seek God's healing grace.

Prayer

God, we give thanks for all that we receive at your table of grace. You prepare this table for us in amazing ways, in times of despair and loneliness, in seasons of doubt and pain, and even in the presence of our enemies. Good Shepherd, gracious Lord, hear our prayers today, for we are thanking you now—in the name of Jesus. Amen.

March 6 / Lent 4

Colossians 2:18-19

Do not let anyone disqualify you, insisting on self-abasement and worship of angels, dwelling on visions, puffed up without cause by a human way of thinking, and not holding fast to the head, from whom the whole body, nourished and held together by its ligaments and sinews, grows with a growth that is from God.

To ponder

As life goes on, it becomes clearer and clearer that the cross is ... the one hope we have that our own lives can move through difficulty to triumph. It's the one thing that enables us to hang on and not give up when hanging on seems impossible and giving up seems imperative. . . . The cross says very clearly that

54

things will work out if we work them out and that whatever is, is important to our life's fulfillment. The cross says that we can rise if we can only endure. —Joan Chittister, *Wisdom Distilled from the Daily*

We grow inward, then outward

Spiritual disciplines are good for us. It may seem at first that making time for daily prayer and Bible reading, meditation, writing, fasting, or voluntary service is meant to distinguish us as "serious Christians" and confer upon us visible credentials of spiritual maturity. God doesn't see it this way at all. In every season of our lives, in every set of circumstances, in every challenge, every setback, every breakthrough, and every joy, the ways we nurture our faith reflect the mysterious power of the cross of Christ. There's nothing "puffed up" about living with an attitude of gratitude, and there's nothing vain or arrogant in expressing a desire to grow in Christ by turning toward God with acts of praise, service, and devotion.

Prayer

All our journeys begin and end in you, God. As we seek to hear and understand the mystery of your voice, encourage us with signs of your faithful presence. Make us stronger in faith and wiser in spirit so we can lift high the cross of Christ and tell the world great stories of your love. Amen.

March 7

Colossians 2:20-21

If with Christ you died to the elemental spirits of the universe, why do you live as if you still belonged to the world? Why do you submit to regulations, "Do not handle, Do not taste, Do not touch"?

To ponder

Prayer is a serene force at work within human beings, stirring them up, changing their hearts, never allowing them to close their eyes in the face of evil, of wars, of all that threatens the innocent of this world. From it we draw the energy to wage other struggles, to transform the human condition and to make the earth a place fit to live in.

All who walk in the footsteps of Christ, while holding themselves in the presence of God, remain alongside other people as well. They do not separate prayer and solidarity with others.
—Brother Roger of Taizé, *Prayer for Each Day*

Prayer empowers a new life

Scripture reminds us that God wants us to live a new life that is shaped and empowered by the love of Christ—and God wants us to let others see what our new life in Christ looks like, sounds like, and feels like. Through the power of prayer, we discover many ways to live out this new life as we serve God in a world wounded by the power of sin and death.

Because we belong to Christ, we are free to take risks, embrace cultural diversity, stand up to injustice, and become healers and peacemakers. As we experience this new life, our lives are forever changed by those we learn to love as Christ has loved us.

Prayer

We praise you, God, for your wondrous power at work in our hearts and in our world. Because of your love, we find friendship and kinship with people near and far. We are free to dream and free even to fail. Thank you for this freedom to live as your sons and daughters. Amen.

March 8

Colossians 2:22-23

All these regulations refer to things that perish with use; they are simply human commands and teachings. These have indeed an appearance of wisdom in promoting self-imposed piety, humility, and severe treatment of the body, but they are of no value in checking self-indulgence.

To ponder

If we remove ourselves from our real and passionate lives . . . then, like all captured creatures, we fall into a sadness that leads to an obsessive yearning. . . . Thereafter, we are at risk of seizing the first thing that promises to make us feel alive again. It is important to keep our eyes open and to carefully weigh offers of an easier existence, a trouble-free path, especially if, in exchange, we are asked to surrender our personal creative joy to a cremating fire rather than enkindling one of our own making. —Clarissa Pinkola Estés, *Women Who Run with the Wolves*

Walking together is far better

If we feel trapped or ensnared, it's good for us to cry out for help. But when the source of our entrapment is hidden from us, we may not realize that we are being limited, oppressed, and denied access to our full potential. Perhaps nothing is worse than being deceived by something that comes into our lives with "an appearance of wisdom."

As God's people, we are church—together. We discover our true selves as we explore the depths of what we share in Christ. Surely we can help each other recognize and resist the seductive powers of false and empty promises. We can encourage one another as we pray together for the Holy Spirit to give us direction and greater understanding. Most of all, we can offer each other the resilient gift of love, because the love we share in Christ sets us free to live our lives fully, with passion and with grace.

Prayer

God, so often you wait for us to recognize the help and support you have already provided. Open our hearts to the wisdom and spiritual gifts of loved ones, companions, and friends. Encourage us today with signs of your abiding presence so that we may grow strong as the body of Christ. Amen.

March 9

Colossians 3:23-24

Whatever your task, put yourselves into it, as done for the Lord and not for your masters, since you know that from the Lord you will receive the inheritance as your reward; you serve the Lord Christ.

To ponder

There will never come a time in life when all things are just like you'd like for them to be. If you are waiting for your life to be just right, you never will do anything with what God has given you.... If ... you have hidden your talent in the earth, go and dig it up! Go now! Go at once! Go as you are.... Go and use what God has given you! —Cleophus J. LaRue, *I Believe I'll Testify*

Our ministries matter

Right on time, right on target. That's how we want our programs and ministries to unfold. Even though we would prefer to have goals that can easily be achieved, God continues to call us to difficult and complex tasks. Why does God call us to confront war and poverty when our world seems so completely enmeshed in violence and economic inequality? Why does God call us to keep forgiving those who hurt us as we work to heal and restore our broken world? Isn't this asking too much?

Today we remember Jesus' great promise: I am with you always, working beside you, within you, and even ahead of you—making all things possible in the wonders of God's reign. Jesus has made us an essential part of his church, and he is present in the ministries entrusted to us. Don't be discouraged; in Christ we can do great things—in God's time and in God's way.

Prayer

God, show us how to persevere, to keep going, to never give up. Keep our eyes on the prize. Strengthen us to do your will. Inspire us with a renewed sense of purpose so that our service will bring honor to your holy name. Amen.

March 10

Colossians 4:2
Devote yourselves to prayer, keeping alert in it with thanksgiving.

To ponder
Through the screaming wind they heard things crashing and things hurtling and dashing with unbelievable velocity. A baby rabbit, terror ridden, squirmed through a hole in the floor and squatted off there in the shadows against the wall, seeming to know that nobody wanted its flesh at such a time. . . .

    The wind came back with triple fury, and put out the light for the last time. They sat in company with the others in other shanties, their eyes straining against crude walls and their souls asking if He meant to measure their puny wills against His. They seemed to be staring at the dark, but their eyes were watching God. —Zora Neale Hurston, *Their Eyes Were Watching God*

Pray every day

A local congregation posted this message on the church sign: "Is prayer your steering wheel or your spare tire?" The power of prayer can never be measured or fully understood, but can you imagine life without it? Prayer allows us to experience God's presence by talking to God and listening for God. Our Lord Jesus prayed constantly, and he calls us to live together as a people who pray.

There are many ways to pray: kneeling, standing, sitting, singing, whispering, crying, with eyes open and with eyes closed, and even groaning with sounds that make sense only to God. Find ways that work for you and pray every day.

Prayer

Faithful God, you delight in all the ways we are able to pray. Bless us with a strong desire to come to you in prayer when we are with others and when we are alone. Hear us as we pray, and bless us as we hear from you. Amen.

March 11

Colossians 4:3-4

At the same time pray for us as well that God will open to us a door for the word, that we may declare the mystery of Christ, for which I am in prison, so that I may reveal it clearly, as I should.

To ponder

Next time you are in a Lutheran worship service, notice what happens when we read the Gospel lesson on Sunday morning. Immediately after the lesson is read, everyone responds, "Praise to you, O Christ!" They do not say, "Praise to you, O Bible!" There is a reason for that.

I tell my students at Trinity Lutheran Seminary: I hope you love the Bible, but remember this—the Bible will never love you back. Jesus will. It is Jesus who loves you, not the Bible. You cannot have a relationship with the Bible. You can have a relationship with Jesus. —Mark Allan Powell, *Opening the Book of Faith*

Open hearts become open doors

Think about some doors that you have seen or used in the last twenty-four hours—creaky doors, doors you had to unlock, automatic glass doors that swung open by themselves, heavy doors on rusty hinges that were difficult to move.

The Bible is like a door—a door to a relationship with Jesus. The grace of God opens our hearts and minds, making the words of scripture come alive and filling us with the love of Christ. As our relationship with Christ deepens, God directs us to new doors of ministry and calls us to take the word into the world. God goes before us in this journey, opening doors so that people hear and come to faith and follow Jesus.

Prayer

Come, Holy Spirit, and fill our hearts with faith and courage as we hear the word of God. May the pages of scripture reveal to us the mysteries of Christ's redeeming love. Open wide the door for your word that we may announce to all the joys of your reign. Amen.

March 12

Colossians 4:5

Conduct yourselves wisely toward outsiders, making the most of the time.

To ponder

Faith is a mission whose end you will only know when you get there, and you will not be responsible for its success, for you will not find it, it will find you. . . . Your mission is not yours, it is . . . a promise that will lead you to places you had never known or ever expected to reach . . . a stranger's smile, an unfamiliar couch to sit on, a bench in the park to share with a friend.
—Vitor Westhelle, *Word in Words: Musings of the Gospel*

No longer strangers

The power of our faith can be seen in the ways we discover new worlds filled with new signs of God's wondrous presence. Old things pass away, and new things appear—especially new people to call friends, new places to call home, and new ways to celebrate the gift of life.

In Christ, we are called to embrace new worlds filled with new faces and new stories of grace. God sends us away from our comfort zones into new relationships so that we may encounter Christ as others tell their stories of grace. The outsiders we meet along the way may well become companions in ministry, sisters and brothers we grow to love as God works in mysterious ways to make us one.

Prayer

Faithful God, what friends we have in Jesus. Thank you for the companions and friends you have sent to bless us through the seasons of our lives. Thank you for sisters and brothers we encounter in the most unusual ways. Your ways are not our ways. You move in mystery, serendipity, and surprise. We praise you for loving us and leading us into worlds unknown to us to find joy among people who share our love for you. Amen.

March 13 / Lent 5

Colossians 4:6

Let your speech always be gracious, seasoned with salt, so that you may know how you ought to answer everyone.

To ponder

Have you ever been in a regional or city disaster caused by flood, earthquake, or fire? At such a time everybody becomes involved—the ne'er-do-well, the people beyond the tracks, the rich, the poor, the good, the bad. This is the moment of judgment and all must be present and accounted for. —Howard Thurman, *The Inward Journey*

We dare to speak in the name of the Lord

An old hymn of the church calls the faithful to "stand up for Jesus." We cannot avoid this sense of accountability to our Lord, because our thoughts, words, and deeds always in some way reflect how Christ is present in our lives. He is the salt that seasons us, and in turn he calls us to live as the salt of the earth—impacting the world around us in ways great and small.

Ask Christ to inspire your speech—as well as your actions—and trust him to season your faith with the wonders of his amazing grace.

Prayer

We come before you on this day that is full of grace. We are grateful for opportunities to serve as instruments of your redeeming love. Your Holy Spirit makes us bold to stand and speak in your name. Keep us steadfast and secure in your promise to work in us and through us so that your will may be done among us. Amen.

March 14

Colossians 3:1

So if you have been raised with Christ, seek the things that are above, where Christ is, seated at the right hand of God.

To ponder

Holiness is a concept that makes ordinary people nervous. Perhaps the uneasiness occurs because the word implies a certain level of impossibility. . . . The holiness that Jesus describes has less to do with pious character traits and more to do with the hosting of God's abiding presence. It is not effort but invitation that opens the human spirit to the possibility that God may sojourn with us. —Barbara A. Holmes, *Joy Unspeakable*

Love is heaven's glory on earth

The mysteries of heaven are vast indeed, but our faith gives us confidence that because of Christ, the power of heaven is also here, in our hearts, in our homes, in our worship, and in our ministries.

This is the great miracle of God's amazing grace: the Holy Spirit abides in the hearts of people of faith. Instead of turning from God in fear and shame, we open our spirits to God's mysterious presence. We connect with the things that are above in all the ways we serve others in Jesus' name. All of God's people discover how heaven's glory is real and available to us through the love of Christ.

Prayer

Divine Savior, your love transcends the boundaries of heaven and earth. Wherever we find you, heaven's glory appears. Wherever your word is preached, the earth rejoices. Wherever we find ourselves today, speak to our hearts, encourage our faith, and lift our spirits to the heavenly places where peace abounds and love never ends. Abide with us and bless us we pray. Amen.

March 15

Colossians 3:2-3

Set your minds on things that are above, not on things that are on earth, for you have died, and your life is hidden with Christ in God.

To ponder

Love is divine only and difficult always. If you think it is easy you are a fool. . . . It is a learned application without reason or motive except that it is God. . . . Love is not a gift. It is a diploma . . . conferring certain privileges: the privilege of expressing love and the privilege of receiving it. How do you know you have graduated? You don't. What you do know is that you are human and therefore educable, and therefore capable of learning how to learn, and therefore interesting to God. . . . God is not interested in you. [God] is interested in love and the bliss it brings to those who understand and share that interest. —Toni Morrison, *Paradise*

Yes, Jesus loves me

Toni Morrison has created a character, a pastor who is very suspicious of the motives behind a certain couple's decision to marry. The minister offers some stinging remarks at the wedding, and all who hear them struggle to understand what he's really saying.

God is love, and God loves us. Even as we struggle to take this in, let alone understand it, God gives us new life shaped by "things that are above" and renewed every day by the love of Christ.

Prayer

We have died to the foolish illusions of this world, and by your grace we have found new life in the power of Christ's love. Strengthen our faith in his promises, and encourage us always to trust in his holy and perfect gifts. Amen.

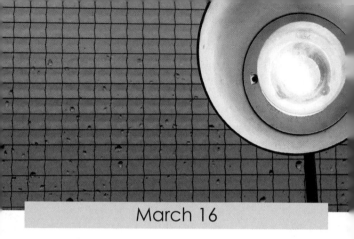

March 16

Colossians 3:4
When Christ who is your life is revealed, then you also will be revealed with him in glory.

To ponder
It is one of the most peculiar things . . . to come together week after week with no intention of being useful or productive, but only of facing an ornate wall to declare things [we] cannot prove about a God [we] cannot see. Our word for it is worship. . . . This is how we learn where we fit. This is how we locate ourselves between the past and the future, between our hopes and our fears, between the earth and the stars. This is how we learn who we are and what we are supposed to be doing: by coming

together to sing and to pray, to be silent and to be still, by peering into the darkness together and telling each other what we see when we do. —Barbara Brown Taylor, *Gospel Medicine*

Softly and tenderly Jesus still calls us

If faithful living was all about some heroic individual accomplishment that we had to figure out on our own, most of us would simply drop out and run away. Our doubts and fears would easily overwhelm our trust in Christ.

The good news is that God calls us to community—often united more by questions than by certainties—a body of people who gather together and listen side by side for the voice of God. We gather and worship because God is revealed—sometimes in bits and pieces, sometimes strengthening us in our sorrows and weaknesses, sometimes causing great joy and ecstasy, sometimes giving clear direction, and sometimes encouraging us to have patience as we wait on the Lord.

Prayer

God, apart from you, we can do nothing. That is why we worship you. Hear our prayers, receive our praises, cleanse our hearts, and reveal to us the splendor of your love. We are unified in our hunger and thirst for signs of your kingdom's glory. Come and fill our hearts with your peace. Amen.

March 17

Colossians 3:5-6

Put to death, therefore, whatever in you is earthly: fornication, impurity, passion, evil desire, and greed (which is idolatry). On account of these the wrath of God is coming on those who are disobedient.

To ponder

We do not set out as those who seek but as those who have been found. The goodness we experience is there already long before. . . . The more we let go of our false desires and needs, the more we . . . come closer to what ancient mysticism called "being apart," which is living out concretely one's farewell to the customs and norms of one's culture. —Dorothee Soelle, *The Silent Cry*

Death brings endings and beginnings

Some might call death the "*d* word," because we try to avoid it. It's too painful and too final to embrace. Some of us accept it only with great sadness and remorse. Death, however, gives us a way to speak wisely about how things change. Death pushes us to recognize how endings and beginnings find balance. The love of Christ finds expression even in death, especially in death, and those who follow him walk a path filled with change and marked by endings and new beginnings.

This *d* word has a place in our faith conversation—because as Christ lives in our hearts, we are sure to change, sure to die, and sure to discover the wonders of a new life.

Prayer

God of resurrection power, we rejoice in the faith that calls us to follow Jesus wherever he leads. Be with us on the mountains, in the valleys, and at the cross. In all the circumstances of our lives, we want to live more and more like him. Every day, let us rise with him, in him, and through him. Amen.

March 18

Colossians 3:7-8

These are the ways you also once followed, when you were living that life. But now you must get rid of all such things—anger, wrath, malice, slander, and abusive language from your mouth.

To ponder

A highly placed white judge is invited to the black church of his family's housekeeper, where he participates in the [Maundy Thursday] foot-washing. As he is washing the housekeeper's feet, he thinks of the countless times she bathed his own children, washing them and kissing them, and is moved to kiss her feet. . . . The South African judge . . . is not thinking of his own piety or liberalness at all, only of the other, who has served so long and whom he now has a chance to serve. . . . He is not merely laying his privilege on the shelf, whence he can easily pick it up again; he is laying it on the line. —Elaine Ramshaw, *Ritual and Pastoral Care*

God loves me as I am, and as I will be

Today's scripture reading reminds us that the habits and patterns of living apart from Christ are all too easy for us to fall into. And yet God calls us into new life in Christ. How is this possible?

In laying it all on the line for us, Jesus teaches us new ways to live and love and give ourselves in service to others. Look at yourself in the mirror, and remember: God is able to change you and create something powerfully new in you. Trust this. Live this. Don't give up on Jesus' promise to make your life new as you live in him with faith, hope, and love.

Prayer

Loving God, you reach out to us, even when we are far from you. You embrace us with the healing power of your love, and you call us to become a part of your healing presence in this world. You claim us, broken and wounded, and through miracles of grace we become instruments of your peace. From the depths of our souls, we thank you and we praise you. Amen.

March 19

Colossians 3:9-10

Do not lie to one another, seeing that you have stripped off the old self with its practices and have clothed yourselves with the new self, which is being renewed in knowledge according to the image of its creator.

To ponder

If I were looking for God, every event and every moment would sow, in my will, grains of His life. . . . For it is God's love that warms me in the sun and God's love that sends the cold rain. . . . It is the love of God that sends the winter days when I am cold and sick, and the hot summer days when I labor. . . . It is God's love that speaks to me in the birds and streams; but also behind the clamor of the city. . . . If these seeds would take root . . .

I would become the love He is. —Thomas Merton, *New Seeds of Contemplation*

As rain falls

I love the rain, especially at night. I lie in bed and hear it on the roof. Sometimes there are only a few intermittent drops, and I wait, hoping for it to fall in a steady pace that calms my heart.

I feel peace as the house covers me and the waters surround me. I am one with it all—the rhythm of the rain; the earth and trees washed fresh, drinking in life; the street rinsed clean; the hum of tires on I-355. All of it encompassed in the rain's embrace.

I feel myself within you, Holy One. I don't know how or why. I just know I am not separate but in you, fresh and renewed, part of the Love and Life you are—wanted, welcome, and treasured, encompassed in the Love who waters the earth and gives life to all that lives.

I hear the rain, Loving Mystery, and I know you, knowing myself, too. I am not what I do, what I think, or what I have accomplished. These are but the clothes in which I hide my nakedness. I am a drop of rain in the shower of your love.

Prayer

As rains fall from the heavens to renew the earth, renew our hearts, O Lord, that each day may be fresh and new. Amen.

Colossians 3:11

In that renewal there is no longer Greek and Jew, circumcised and uncircumcised, barbarian, Scythian, slave and free; but Christ is all and in all!

To ponder

Christ empties himself, not only in the Incarnation, but also on the cross, and is now incarnate through the Breath of God animating the Body, the church. The manifestation of Christ continues to show forth in the church and its various activities which constitute its mission of being and building a communion in the One Love. —Michael Downey, *Altogether Gift*

One Love

A married couple recently joined our congregation, seeking baptism for their two children. Rejected in some circles, they were searching for a community of grace, a place where they could find a welcome. The mother asked if she should cover her tattoos the day of the service. She didn't want to suffer further rejection or distract attention from the baptism. The serenity prayer was tattooed on her ankle; the baby's feet were inked on her arm.

When the day came, joy and welcome filled the sanctuary.

They are your gift to us, Holy One, sent to show your grace and reveal the mystery of what you are doing among us and in all creation. You are the Love who transcends every human boundary. You are the hunger in our hearts to be joined in one love—the Love you are—beyond all that separates.

Black and white, rich and poor, progressives and conservatives, young and old, singles and married—you join us as one that your love may be all in all, a communion of grace.

Prayer

Make us one, joined heart to heart in your heart, sharing the One Love you are. Amen.

March 21

Colossians 3:12
As God's chosen ones, holy and beloved, clothe yourselves with compassion, kindness, humility, meekness, and patience.

To ponder
If any of you have ever been to a Greek wedding, you may have seen their distinctive way of dancing. . . . It's called perichoresis. There are . . . at least three [dancers]. They start . . . weaving in and out in this very beautiful pattern of motion. They . . . go faster and faster . . . staying in perfect rhythm and in sync with each other. Eventually, they are dancing so quickly . . . that as you look at them, it becomes a blur. Their individual identities are part of a larger dance. The early church fathers and mothers looked at that dance and said, "That's what the Trinity is like."

It's a harmonious set of relationships . . . mutual giving and
receiving. . . . The perichoresis is the dance of love.
—Jonathan Marlowe, "The Dance of Love: Perichoresis"

Lily's dance

Lily dances with delight as we sing, "Glory to God in the
highest." She steps into the aisle with a little girl twirl as the
congregation lifts praise: "Holy, holy, holy." Her feet are made for
joy and her soul for delight.

Greater still is the delight I feel as I watch and coax her to
come to the Lord's Table where I stand, hoping the congregation
will see her and feel what I feel.

This is what you want for us, Jesus. You want us to know this
delight of love, the joy of knowing and praising you. Watching
her, I am clothed with the life you want for me. Love and compassion, kindness and humility flow from my heart as naturally
as laughter from the lips of a loved child.

You ache for me to know and become the beauty I see in this
girl, barely three. And you invite us always to come close and be
clothed in the life you give, dearest Christ, the life you are.

And in this moment I see *exactly* what you are and what you
give us . . . in Lily's dance.

Prayer

Awaken joy in our souls, Holy One, and clothe us in your kindness that our lives may be a light of grace and beauty. Amen.

March 22

Colossians 3:13

Bear with one another and, if anyone has a complaint against another, forgive each other; just as the Lord has forgiven you, so you also must forgive.

To ponder

Alas . . . the church has always had a tough time latching on to [this] truth. . . . The church gives (and, worst of all, the world understands it to be giving) the clear impression that grace works only on the early birds and eager beavers who cooperate with it. But that's dead wrong. Grace works without requiring *anything* on our part. It's not expensive. It's not even cheap. It's *free*. Our enjoyment of grace, of course, is another matter.
—Robert Farrar Capon, *The Romance of the Word*

Stop counting

I don't think there is arithmetic in the kingdom of heaven. You don't count our sins and failures, Jesus. And you tell us not to count our own or anybody else's, for that matter. Today is a new day, you say. Let go of what was and *live*, free from the need to keep score.

We love to keep score; all kinds of games depend on it, and we like to see that our score is a little better than that of others. So we keep score with money or by comparing how our children or grandkids are doing.

Some even keep score with religion, pretending they—or their church—are bigger, better, or "more spiritual."

But you are not the Eternal Bookkeeper giving demerits and passing out spiritual merit badges. You take away the sins of *the world*. They're gone. Kaput. Every last one of them. Forgiven.

Sounds *crazy*, but that's the way your plan works. You are joining everything in one great communion of grace in which everyone belongs because you love and forgive them all. The only people who risk excluding themselves are those who are too busy counting other people's faults to come to the party.

Prayer

Teach us not to count our wrongs or those of others, lest our differences tear us apart. Amen.

Colossians 3:14

Above all, clothe yourselves with love, which binds everything together in perfect harmony.

To ponder

Indeed, in his words and deeds Jesus embodies God's intention for the world now and to come, a world transfigured in and by Love. Jesus' life was not a free and easy ride, but a continual struggle against injustice and hate, illness, suffering, and depersonalization. The reign of God, God's intention for the world now and to come, is realized only in a communion in the One Love, which Jesus manifests most fully at the table on the night before he dies and in his self-giving on the cross. —Michael Downey, *Altogether Gift*

Folded together

I have a favorite image of Ethan, my youngest grandson. He is seven and getting bigger, but not too big to curl up next to his mother, my daughter. With him folded into her side, they are like one person, an exquisite unity of love and comfort, together.

Sometimes Ethan does the same thing with his big brother Ben, and he often takes Ben's hand as they walk down the street. Brothers as one.

It touches me, Holy One. I see in them the union of love that you intend for all things, a picture of the harmony and mutual affection into which you draw us and all that is.

They show me the life I am to live and the love I am to love. I see them and hear your invitation to fold myself into your side.

"Come find yourself in the Love I am," you say. "Only then will you know the joy I long to give you. Only then will you be clothed in the love that holds my people together as one; only then will you know the loving communion that will hold *everything*, *everyone*, *everywhere* in a great sea of grace.

"Only then will you know me."

Prayer

Clothe us, O Lord, in the Love you are, that we may be one with all you love. Amen.

March 24 / Maundy Thursday

Colossians 3:15
And let the peace of Christ rule in your hearts, to which indeed you were called in the one body. And be thankful.

To ponder
Peace is a deep disposition of the heart. It is an ability to let go of the need to be right, an ability based on the knowledge that our rightness or wrongness in any issue is irrelevant to God's love for us and our neighbor. The peace that comes with claiming ourselves in God is the foundation of our ability to love others in the most humble places and everyday ways. —Roberta Bondi, *To Pray and to Love*

Aah

There are weary sighs and sighs that come only when one arrives home, wherever or *whoever* that is.

A deep *aah* passes from lungs through lips when one *finally* rests in a great love that is always there, a love that wants and welcomes you to be nothing but yourself, a love that hungers for your nearness simply to savor the joy of being together.

Is this an unseemly way to speak of you, Jesus? Too familiar, perhaps?

I don't think so. You opened your arms to bless children and receive beggars, lepers, and others no right-minded person would touch.

On the cross, you opened your arms in one great divine embrace of me and all that is. You take me into yourself, all I am and ever will be, beckoning me to come home and know the Love who wants me, the Love who never lets go but is always there.

In your embrace, the deep sigh of my heart finds release, for I am home. But not just me. You welcome everyone everywhere into your embrace to know the peace of belonging to you, one people joined in your grace, finally home.

Aah.

Prayer

You are our peace, O Lord. Fill our hearts with the peace of being home, together, in you. Amen.

March 25 / Good Friday

Colossians 3:16

Let the word of Christ dwell in you richly; teach and admonish one another in all wisdom; and with gratitude in your hearts sing psalms, hymns, and spiritual songs to God.

To ponder

The incarnation is God giving God's self to humanity and creation. . . . The incarnation did not take place because of human sin. Rather, the incarnation was the affirmation of the goodness of the created world and God's wanting to bring that work to completion in Jesus. . . . There is a creation so that there can be a divine embodiment of love, and the incarnation is God's embrace of creation, and of the human condition in particular.
—Michael W. Blastic, "Attentive Compassion"

Yes, good

What word do you speak on this day we call *Good* Friday? This cross, is there anything good about it?

Even today, barbarous hands lift desperate souls onto crosses to terrify populations with the limp bodies of their victims. Good? This? How do we give thanks when those who call on your name are brutalized in ancient lands?

Yet we do, Jesus, for on the cross you chose us. You chose this conflicted world, our brutal history, becoming one with us: one with our sorrows, one with our fears and pains, one with our joys and celebrations, sharing all we are that you might share all you are with us.

On the cross you embrace the worst of what the world can do, the darkest places in our hearts, and you say, "Yes, it is *this* troubled world that I love. I choose you. I choose this that we might be one as the Father and I are one.

"On this day you call *good*, I take all that you are—and all that is—into myself that you may know the Love I am, the Heart who hungers for you. Welcome home."

Prayer

God, fill our hearts with the unfailing "yes" of your love that we may sing your praise with grateful hearts and unfailing hope. Amen.

March 26 / Resurrection of Our Lord

Colossians 3:17

And whatever you do, in word or deed, do everything in the name of the Lord Jesus, giving thanks to God the Father through him.

To ponder

The Christian hope is . . . the hope of resurrection. . . . If we are seized by the spirit of the resurrection, we get up out of our sadness and apathy. We begin to flower and become fruitful again, like plants and trees in the spring of the year. An untamed love for life awakens in us; we drive out the sweet poison of resignation, and our painful remembrances of death are healed. We encounter life again like children, in eager expectation. —Jürgen Moltmann, *The Source of Life*

It's morning

Morning comes with cobalt sky and life budding new. The bees, busy with their work, are a portrait of hope, obscurely knowing there is sweetness in each blossom, drawing life as gift from each one—grace, simply there.

And so it is that resurrection comes, because it is your nature to give life as gift, eternal life, the life of heaven—now, sweeter still than sun-kissed spring mornings.

Thank you. Yes, I know: the words are entirely inadequate, but my heart requires them. And I know you hunger to hear those words from me for the Love that fills me each time I sing the wonder of your empty tomb.

I believe the wonder of this day, because again and again I encounter the Love that evil and sin, human confusion and apathy cannot kill. The Love who took on flesh continues to take form and flesh in communities of grace where the communion of heart and mind fills human souls with love and hope.

I see and feel it, and know: morning has come. It's a new day, for you live and love. Whatever else the day holds, it holds you, and you hold us all.

It's morning, another day of grace.

Prayer

God, fill me with life eternal that I may live in the newness of your love. Amen.

Notes

February 10: Herbert Brokering, *Surprise Me, Jesus* (Augsburg, 1973), 94. **February 11**: Jürgen Moltmann, *The Source of Life* (Fortress Press, 1997), 40–41. **February 12**: Richard Rohr, *The Naked Now* (Crossroad, 2009), 22. **February 13**: Ilia Delio, "Love at the Heart of the Universe," *Oneing* 1, no. 1 (2013): 22. **February 14**: Roberta Bondi, *To Love as God Loves* (Fortress Press, 1987), 22–23. **February 15**: Christian Wiman, *My Bright Abyss* (Farrar, Strauss and Giroux, 2013), 161. **February 16**: Henri J. M. Nouwen, *Life of the Beloved* (Crossroad, 1992), 45. **February 17**: Thomas Merton, *New Seeds of Contemplation* (New Directions, 1972), 297. **February 18**: Alex Haley, *The Autobiography of Malcolm X* (Ballantine Books, 1964), 340–41. **February 19**: Bruce H. Kramer with Kathy Wurzer, *We Know How This Ends: Living While Dying* (University of Minnesota Press, 2015), 169. **February 20**: Anne Lamott, *Traveling Mercies* (Random House, 1999), 66–67. **February 21**: Dan Savage, *This American Life*, episode 379: "Return to the Scene of the Crime," act 3: "Our Man of Perpetual Sorrow," 2009 (Chicago: Chicago Public Media and Ira Glass); originally aired May 1, 2009. Online transcript: http://www.thisamericanlife.org/radio-archives/episode/379/transcript. **February 22**: Audre Lorde, *The Cancer Journals* (Aunt Lute Books, 1980), 60. **February 23**: Johnny Nash, "I Can See Clearly Now," *I Can See Clearly Now* (Epic Records, 1972). **February 24**: Patrick, 372–466, para. Cecil Frances Alexander, 1823–1895, "I Bind unto Myself Today," *Evangelical Lutheran Worship*, hymn 450. **February 25**: Reinhold Niebuhr, *Leaves from the Notebook of a Tamed Cynic* (John Knox Press, 1929), 47. **February 26**: Václav Havel, "Dear Dr. Husák," in *Open Letters: Selected Writings, 1965–1990* (Vintage, 1992). **February 27**: Noémia da Sousa, "Poem of Distant Childhood," in *Ain't I a Woman! A Book of Women's Poetry from around the World*, ed. Illona Linthwaite (Wings Books, 1987), 16. **February 28**: Walt Whitman, "Song of Myself," in *Leaves of Grass* (Bantam Classic Edition, 1983), 73. **February 29**: Julia Kasdorf, "What I Learned from My Mother," in *Sleeping Preacher* (University of Pittsburgh Press, 1991), 43. **March 1**: Rainer Maria Rilke, *Letters to a Young Poet* (W. W. Norton and Co., 1934), 27. **March 2**: Khaled Hosseini, *The Kite Runner* (Riverhead Books, 2003), 371. **March 3**: Walter Wangerin Jr., *Water, Come Down! The Day You Were Baptized* (Augsburg Fortress, 1999). **March 4**: Parker J. Palmer, *The Company of Strangers* (Crossroad, 1986), 22–23. **March 5**: Michael Yaconelli, *Dangerous Wonder* (NavPress, 1998), 128. **March 6**: Joan Chittister, *Wisdom Distilled from the Daily* (HarperCollins, 1990), 148. **March 7**: Brother Roger of Taizé, in *Prayer for Each Day* (GIA Publications, 1998). **March 8**: Clarissa Pinkola Estés, *Women Who Run with the Wolves* (Ballantine Books, 1992), 228. **March 9**: Cleophus J. LaRue, *I Believe I'll Testify: The Art of African American Preaching* (Westminster John Knox, 2011), 143–44. **March 10**: Zora Neale Hurston, *Their Eyes Were Watching God*, 2nd ed. (University of Illinois, 1978), 235–36. **March 11**: Mark Allan Powell, in *Opening the Book of Faith: Lutheran Insights for Bible Study* (Augsburg Fortress, 2008), 32. **March 12**: Vitor Westhelle, *Word in Words: Musings of the Gospel* (Christava Sahitya Samithy, 2009), 71. **March 13**: Howard Thurman, *The Inward Journey* (Friends United Press, 1971), 74. **March 14**: Barbara A. Holmes, *Joy Unspeakable* (Fortress Press, 2004), 26. **March 15**: Toni Morrison, *Paradise* (Random House, 1997), 141–42. **March 16**: Barbara Brown Taylor, *Gospel Medicine* (Cowley Publications, 1995), 72. **March 17**: Dorothee Soelle, *The Silent Cry: Mysticism and Resistance* (Augsburg Fortress, 2001), 90–92. **March 18**: Elaine Ramshaw, *Ritual and Pastoral Care* (Fortress Press, 1987), 91–92. **March 19**: Thomas Merton, *New Seeds of Contemplation* (New Directions, 1972), 16–17. **March 20**: Michael Downey, *Altogether Gift: A Trinitarian Spirituality* (Orbis, 2000), 92. **March 21**: Jonathan Marlowe, "The Dance of Love: Perichoresis," *Music and Dancing*, https://musicanddancing.wordpress.com/perichoresis. **March 22**: Robert Farrar Capon, *The Romance of the Word* (Eerdmanns, 1995), 10. **March 23**: Michael Downey, *Altogether Gift: A Trinitarian Spirituality* (Orbis, 2000), 85. **March 24**: Roberta Bondi, *To Pray and to Love* (Fortress Press, 1991), 95. **March 25**: Michael W. Blastic, "Attentive Compassion: Franciscan Resources for Ministry," *Handbook of Spirituality for Ministers*, vol. 2, ed. Robert Wicks (Paulist, 2000), 257. **March 26**: Jürgen Moltmann, *The Source of Life* (Fortress Press, 1997), 81.